HEMP BRACELETS FOR BEGINNERS

A COMPLETE BEGINNER'S GUIDE TO LEARN HOW TO BRAID, KNOT AND PRODUCE BEAUTIFUL HANDMADE JEWELRY PATTERNS

JULIEN MANDY

Made with ♥ on the Notion Press Platform
www.notionpress.com

Contents

Title Page

HEMP BRACELETS FOR BEGINNERS

A complete beginner's guide to learn how to braid, knot and produce beautiful handmade jewelry patterns

Julien mandy

CHAPTER ONE

INTRODUCTION TO MACRAME HEMP BRACELETS PATTERNS

In this step-by-step guide, you'll learn how to produce a variety of basic macrame hemp bracelet styles, as well as an easy adjustable closing.

Enter Caption

Hemp bracelets are making a comeback! I recall doing them during my senior and sophomore years of high school and college, and I had no idea I was doing macrame!

These three bracelet designs are quite easy to learn, even if you've never created one before!

In this guide, we'll make macrame hemp bracelets using the beaded square knot, the plain square knot, and the twisted half knot design.

For these bracelets, I used a medium-weight hemp cord. You might create these with a chunkier hemp rope if desired, but bear in mind that you'll need longer cords to begin!

Instructions for Sliding Square Knot Bracelet Closure

I used the same adjustable closure for all three bracelets, and it's quite easy to make!

To avoid repetition, I've included the lesson for the closure in this work. Keep reading.

Enter Caption

Therefore, just follow the guide for the bracelet you choose and go to the bottom to learn how to build the sliding macrame closure!

CHAPTER TWO

BRACELET MADE WITH HEMP AND BEADS

You'll Need the Following Supplies:

- Cord made of hemp
- 1 piece measuring 16 inches in length (center cord)
- 1 piece measuring 70 inches in length (working cords)
- 1 piece measuring 14 inches in length (for slider closure)
- 7 spherical beads with a hole wide enough for the hemp rope to go through (mine were 10 mm)
- a piece of tape or a cork board with t-pins to secure your work
- scissors
- glue for crafts

Stage 1: The first step is to string the beads.

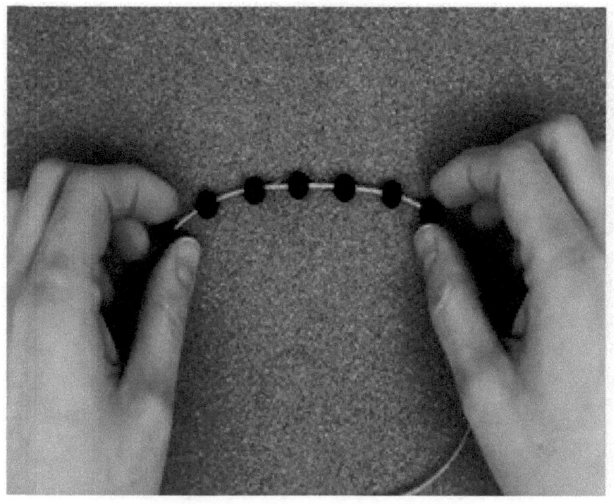

Enter Caption

String the seven beads onto the cord's 16-inch central piece. You need not worry about the spacing; we'll take care of it in a few moments.

Tie an overhand knot at one end of the string and secure it with a T-pin in the middle of the knot to the cork board. (Alternatively, you may just glue it to your desk.)

Stage 2: Tie the Square Knots

Fold the 70-inch-long rope in half and put it beneath the middle cord we just tied to the cork board.

Then tie the first half of a square knot around the middle cord, ensuring that each side of the working cords has an equal length of cable (so it stays centered.)

Enter Caption

Now complete the square knot by tying the other side.

Assure that this initial square knot is pressed up against the previous overhand knot.

Five more square knots. You'll end up with six square knots in total.

Stage 3: Alternating Beads and Knots

Slide one of the beads up against the newly made row of square knots. Then, immediately after the bead, tie two square knots, taking care not to leave any gap between the knots and the bead.

Rep this procedure with the remaining beads, tying two square knots between each one.

Enter Caption

After you've inserted the last bead, tie six additional square knots to complete the design.

Stage 4: Completing the work

Once you've made the last six square knots, tie a half knot on the inside of your bracelet (similar to the first section of the knot when tying your shoes).

Apply a little amount of craft glue to the knot and let it to dry for a few minutes.

Then, near to the knot, cut the working cables. Not to worry, the adhesive will prevent it from unraveling!

If desired, you may apply a little amount of more adhesive to the cut ends and smooth them down.

Trim the remaining two ends of the central cord to the same length, and then secure them with an overhand knot.

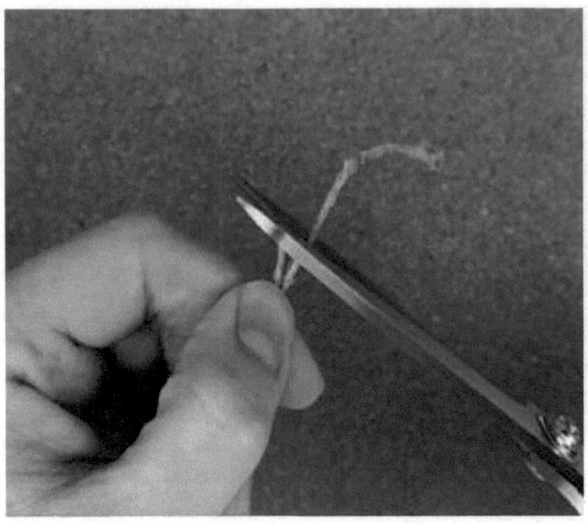

Enter Caption

Make the end cords about three inches long each to allow for the sliding closing.

Scroll down to the last portion of this tutorial to discover how to complete this bracelet with the sliding closure!

CHAPTER THREE

HEMP BRACELET WITH SQUARE KNOTS

You'll Need the Following Supplies:

• Cord made of hemp

• Two 16-inch-long sections (center cords)

• 1 piece measuring 72 inches in length (working cords)

• 1 piece measuring 14 inches in length (for slider closure)

• a piece of tape or a cork board with t-pins to secure your work

• scissors

• glue for crafts

Preparation of Your Cords

Pinning or taping your center cables to a corkboard or to your work area will secure them (like I did here).

Then, as shown in the illustration below, fold your working cable in half and slip it under your center cord.

Enter Caption

Stage 2: Tie the Square Knots

Then, beginning with the middle strands, begin tying square knots around them.

Continue tying until the bracelet reaches the desired length. I created a six-inch square knot sennit.

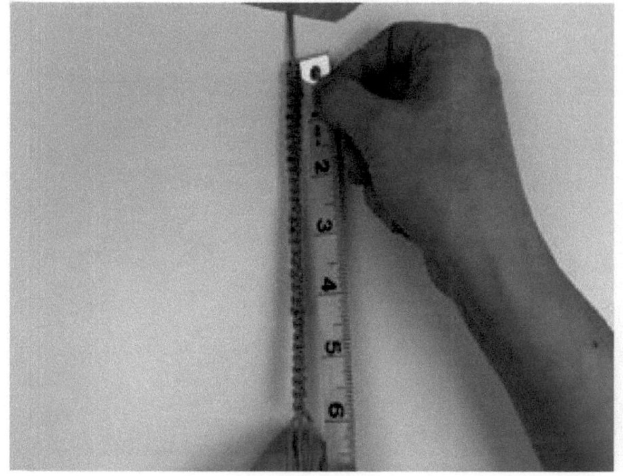

Enter Caption

Stage 3: Completing the work

Once you've made the last six square knots, tie a half knot on the inside of your bracelet (similar to the first section of the knot when tying your shoes).

Apply a little amount of craft glue to the knot and let it to dry for a few minutes.

Then, near to the knot, cut the working cables. Not to worry, the adhesive will prevent it from unraveling!

If desired, you may apply a little amount of more adhesive to the cut ends and smooth them down.

Enter Caption

After trimming the ends to make them equal, tie an overhand knot. Your ends should be around three inches long each.

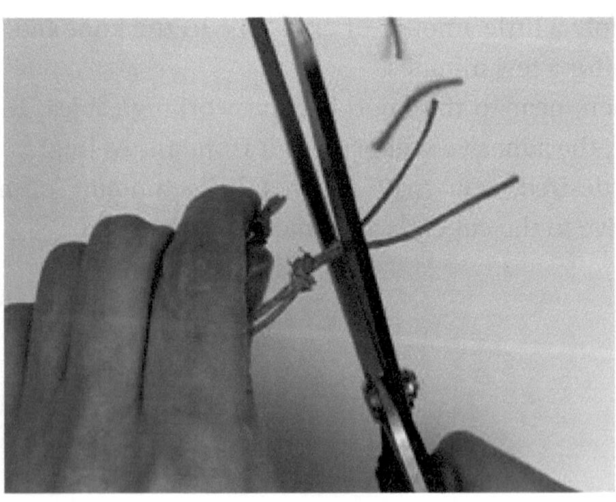

Enter Caption

Scroll down to the last portion of this tutorial to discover how to complete this bracelet with the sliding closure!

CHAPTER FOUR

BRACELET WITH SPIRAL HALF KNOT

You'll Need the Following Supplies:

- Cords made of hemp
- Two 16-inch-long sections (center cords)
- 1 piece measuring 72 inches in length (working cords)
- 1 piece measuring 14 inches in length (for slider closure)
- a piece of tape or a cork board with t-pins to secure your work
- scissors
- glue for crafts

Preparation of Your Cords

Pinning or taping your center cables to a corkboard or to your work area will secure them (like I did here).

Then, as shown in the illustration below, fold your working cable in half and slip it under your center cord.

Stage 2: Spiral Half Knots

Wrap a sennit of spiral half knots around the two central cords to the desired length. Right here is a tutorial on how to perform the spiral half knot.

Mine is around six inches long.

Stage 3: Completing the piece

On the interior of the bracelet, tie the working cord ends in a half knot and secure with glue.

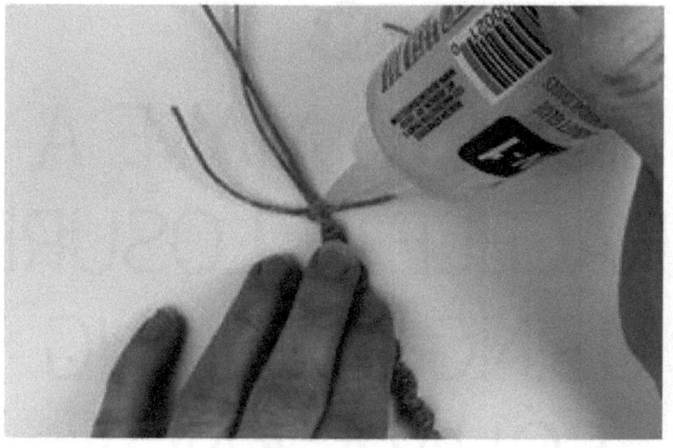

Enter Caption

Cut the string ends close to the knot after it has dried.

Then tie the ends of the center cords together, leaving an equal length of cord on each side, and remove any extra cord.

CHAPTER FIVE

HOW TO MAKE A BRACELET CLOSURE USING A SLIDING SQUARE KNOT

After creating these bracelets, it's time to learn how to make a sliding adjustable square knot closing!

To begin, clasp the bracelet's two sides together, as though it were wrapped around your wrist.

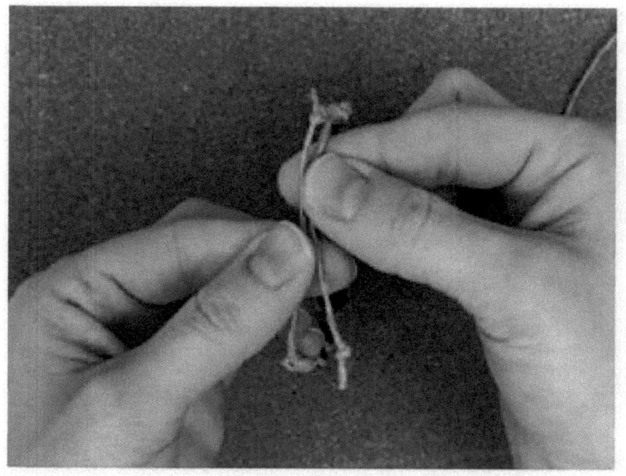

Enter Caption

Then take your 14-inch string and wrap it over the two overlapped strands, forming three square knots.

Once the three square knots are formed, tie a half knot on the inside and bind with a drop of glue.

Take care not to get glue on the middle cords, since this will prevent the knot from sliding.

Enter Caption

Cut the two ends close to the knot after the glue has cured.

In Summation

I hope you liked these designs for macrame hemp bracelets!

CHAPTER SIX

DIY FRIENDSHIP BRACELET

For many months, we've been getting emails seeking a tutorial on how to make a friendship bracelet. To that end, friends, inquire and you will get! Today, we'll walk you through the process of creating the classic chevron design. If you were an expert at making friendship bracelets in elementary school but have since forgotten how, consider this a refresher course. And if you can create them with your eyes closed and your arms tied behind your back... uh... can we still be friends?

You will need the following:

- embroidery floss
- a safety pin or a piece of tape
- an ax and a pair of scissors

To begin, cut several strands of embroidery thread about 24 inches in length. Assure that each color has two sets. Combine the threads and secure them with a knot, allowing at least three inches of slack. Tape or safety pin it to a flat surface or a cushion. Separate the two sets by arranging the strands in a mirror-image manner, with the outermost strands the same color as the innermost strands, and so on inwards.

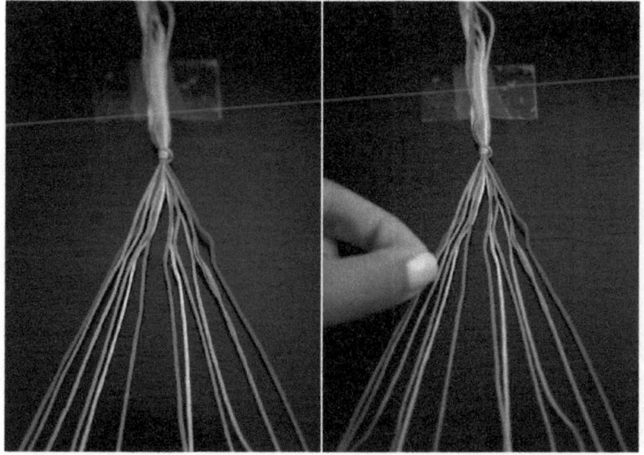

Begin on the left side with the outermost color (red) and create a forward knot by forming a 4-shape over the second color, looping it under and back through the opening.

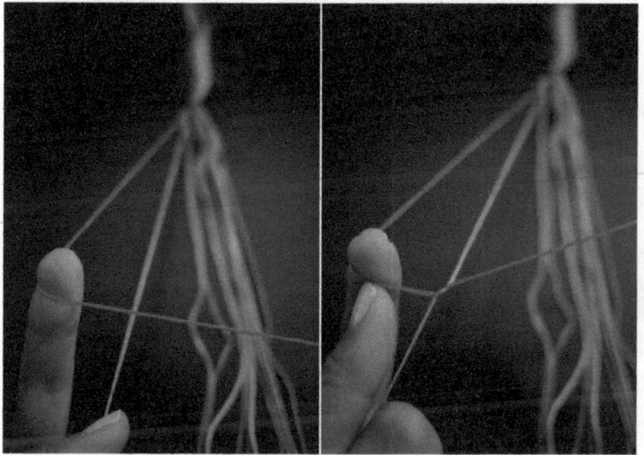

To tighten, pull up and to the right. Twice over each color, tie the same knot. Continue knotting over each color in a clockwise direction until the outermost color reaches the center. This is half of the design for the chevron.

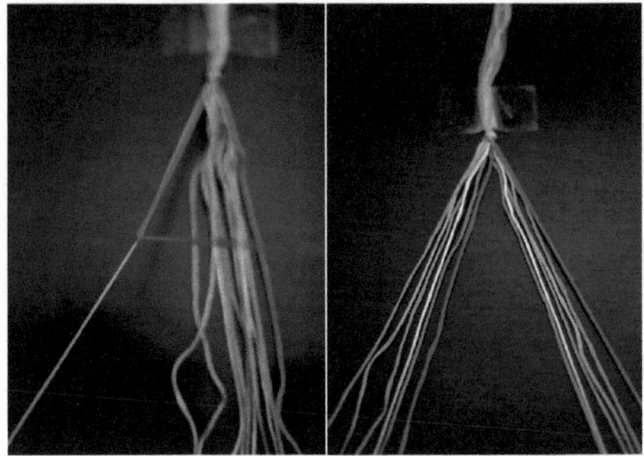

Now, take the outermost color on the right side (shown in red) and tie a backward knot over the second color, looping it under and back through the hole. To tighten, pull up and to the left. Don't forget to double-knot each color!

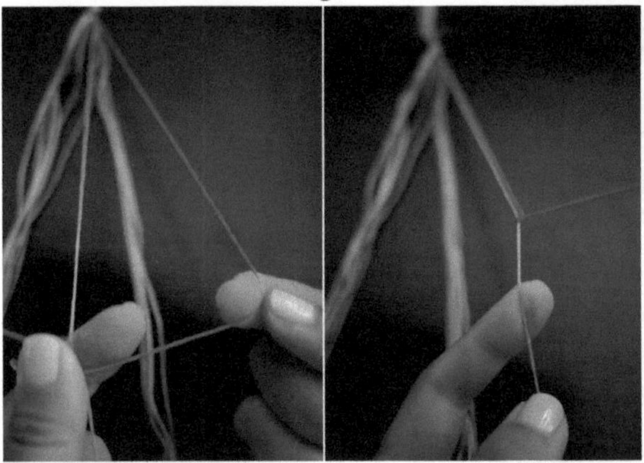

Continue knotting in a left-to-right direction until the outermost strand reaches the center. To join the two pieces, tie a reverse knot using the two center strands. Did you remember to double-knot? The first row of chevrons is now complete! Proceed with the next color, which is now the outermost strand...

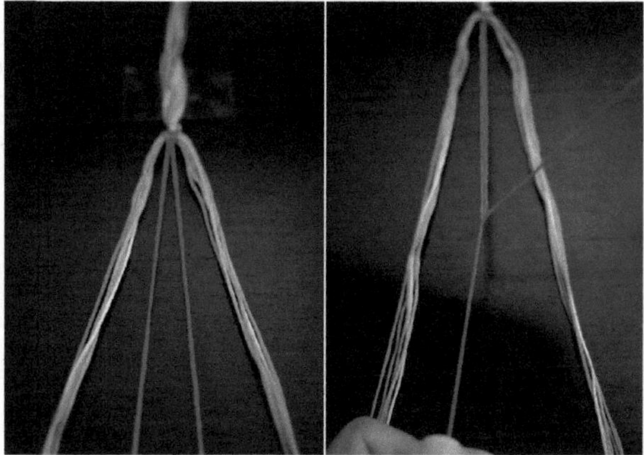

While keeping track of the color sequence is necessary for the first few rows, after the third or fourth row, the strands will naturally fall into place. Complete the look with a knot and a braid.

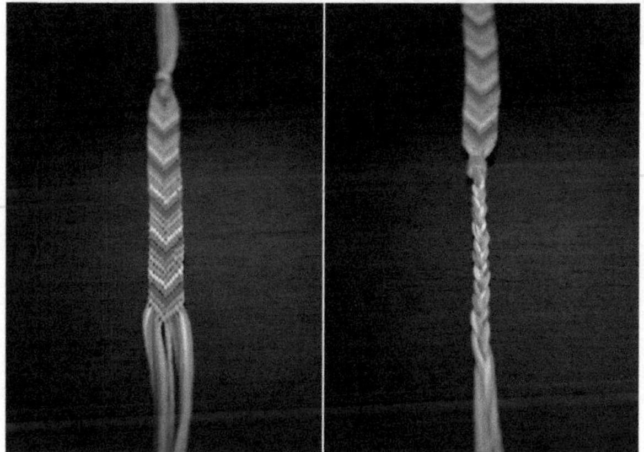

Cut one set of colors and just continue the outermost color all the way to the right side to create a striped bracelet. To create an asymmetrical chevron, combine the colors before splitting them into two groups. Count the amount of strands each time so you know when to stop in the middle. To create an embellished bracelet, take a little length of rhinestone chain and attach it to the top of the bracelet. Then, using an embroidery needle, sew embroidery thread between each rhinestone. A wrist full of Honestly WTF do-it-yourself projects to keep you occupied over the summer!

CHAPTER SEVEN

BRAIDED BEAD BRACELET – (DIY)

It's been quite some time since our previous DIY bracelet. I'm not sure about you, but our wrists have been pleading for another splash of color for months. As a result of experimenting with materials on hand, we've devised a guide for a braided bead bracelet, a close relative of the hex nut and wrap bracelet. Because, quite frankly, one can never have too much...

You will need the following:

- 1.5 yd. waxed linen cord

- 50–70 seed beads size 8/o
- a button with two holes in the range of 10-13mm
- scissors

Cut a 26-inch and a 19-inch length of waxed linen cord. The longer strand should be folded in half. Align the shorter strand's end with both of the longer strand's ends. Excess fabric is folded over the top of the folded piece, forming two parallel loops. (To expand photos, click on them)

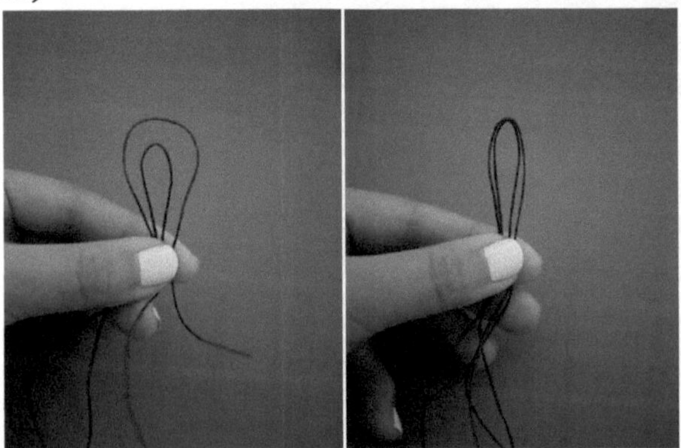

Make a knot around half an inch below the loops. Snip off the additional fourth strand, leaving three equal-length strands.

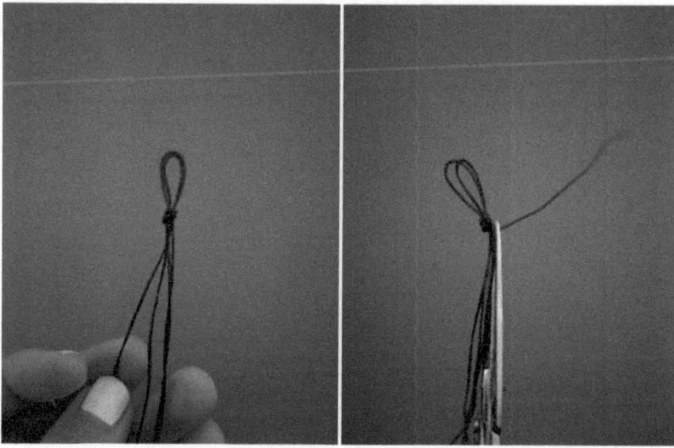

Braid the threads together. Braid in the beads after approximately one inch. A bead should be threaded onto the outer left strand.

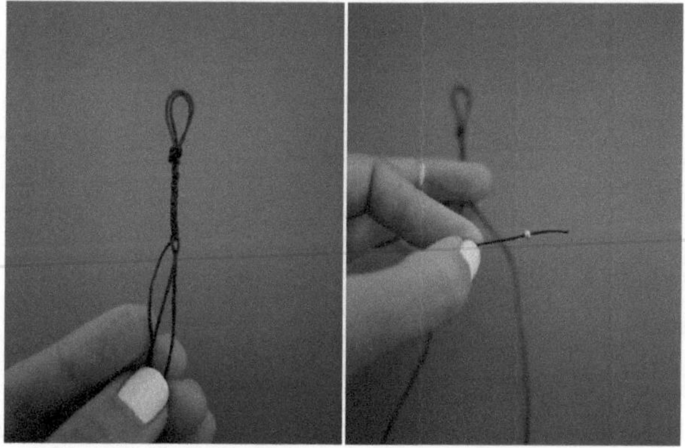

Cross the left strand across the center and push the bead against the braid's base. Thread another bead onto the outer right strand at this point. Cross it at the base of the braid.

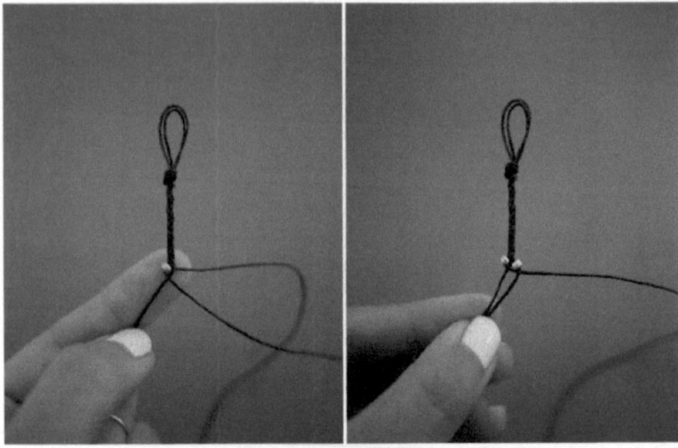

Maintain a finger at the base of the braid to secure the beads and maintain the braid taut. Continue threading beads on before crossing each strand.

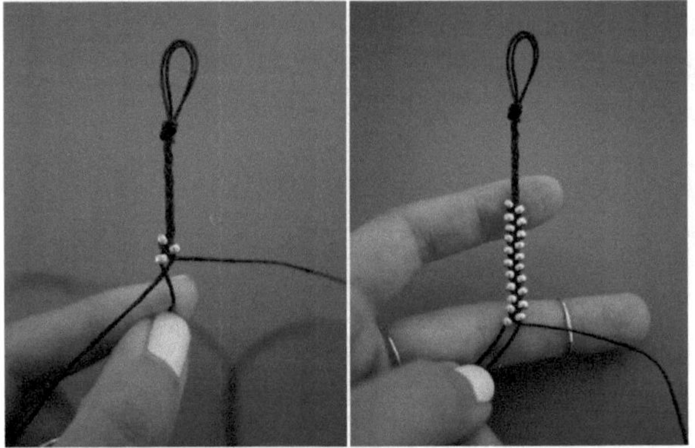

Add another inch of braided string to the bracelet, measuring it against the wrist. Create a knot.

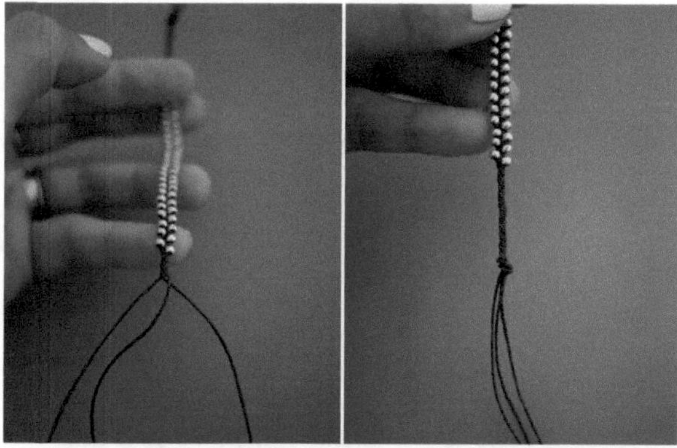

Thread two strands through one hole and one strand through the other hole of a two-hole button. Another knot is used to secure it.

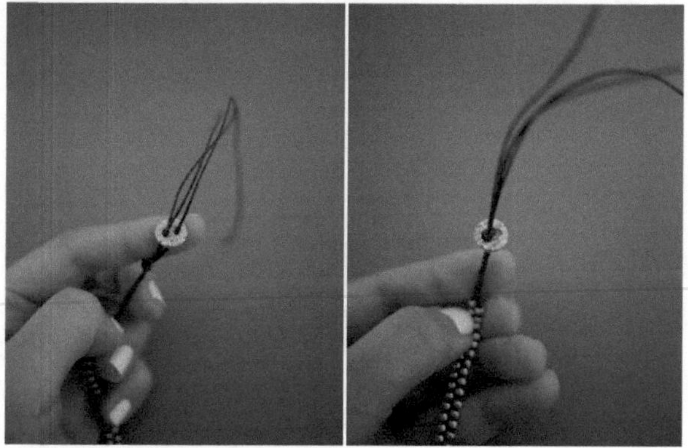

Cut out or trim the end.

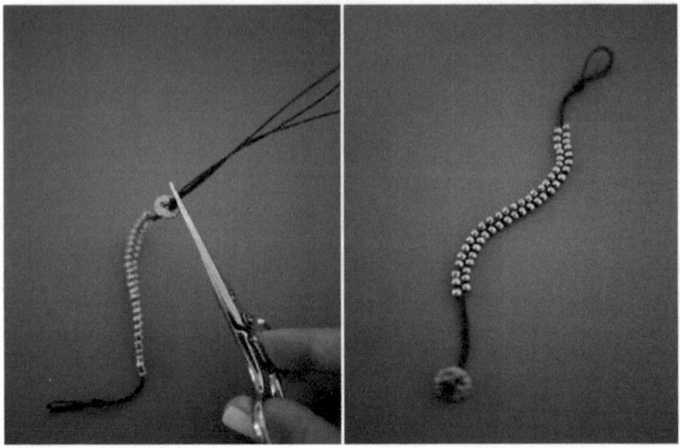

Your bracelet is now complete! Utilize a variety of colored waxed linen and beads.

Stack as you want!

The End

9 798889 864387

Printed by Libri Plureos GmbH in Hamburg,
Germany